101 EASTER JOKES
FOR KIDS

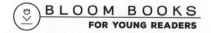
BLOOM BOOKS
FOR YOUNG READERS

Published by:
Bloom Books for Young Readers
an imprint of Ulysses Press
PO Box 3440
Berkeley, CA 94703

ISBN: 978-1-64604-616-4
Library of Congress Control Number: 2023943925

Printed in the United States
2 4 6 8 10 9 7 5 3 1

Image credits: cover art © kotoffei/Shutterstock.com; Easter eggs © Alona_S/Shutterstock.com; page border top © Christos Georghiou/Shutterstock.com; page border bottom © ExpressVectors/Shutterstock.com. Chick in eggshells and conversing Easter egg cartoons created with the assistance of DALL-E.

Why did the Easter egg hide?

He was a little chicken.

How do bunnies get from one vegetable garden to another?

They take a taxi cabbage!

How does the Easter Bunny say Happy Easter?

Hoppy Easter!

Why are Easter eggs so fascinated with outer space?

They want to meet egg-straterrestrials.

What can you call the Easter Bunny when he has the sniffles?

A runny bunny.

What do you call a zen egg?

An ommmmmm-elet.

How do bunnies keep their fur neat?

They use a harebrush.

I was going to tell you
a joke about an Easter
egg... but it's not all
it's cracked up to be!

What did everyone call the Easter Bunny who couldn't remember anything?

They called him a hare-brain.

Why are people always tired in April?

Because they've just finished a March.

Why couldn't the Easter egg family watch cable?

Because their TV was scrambled!

What did the rabbits do after their wedding?

Went on their bunnymoon.

How long does a baby chick celebrate Easter?

Around the cluck!

What is the Easter Bunny's favorite state capital?

Albunny, New York.

What do you need if your chocolate eggs mysteriously disappear?

An eggsplanation.

What is the Easter Bunny's favorite kind of music?

Hip-hop!

What do you get when you cross a frog with a rabbit?

A bunny ribbit.

What do you call a sleeping Easter egg?

Eggs-austed!

Why did the rabbit cross the road?

Because it was the chicken's day off.

How do you know the Easter Bunny is really smart?

Because he's an egghead.

How does a rabbit throw a tantrum?

He gets hopping mad.

**What do you get when
you cross a bunny
with an onion?**

A bunion.

How do rabbits stay cool during the summer?

With hare conditioning.

How can you tell which rabbits are the oldest in a group?

Just look for the gray hares.

What kind of cars do bunnies drive?

Hop rods!

Where does the Easter Bunny go for pancakes?

I. . .HOP.

Where does Valentine's Day come after Easter?

In the dictionary.

What do the Easter Bunny and Michael Jordan have in common?

They're both famous for making baskets.

How does a rabbit make gold soup?

He begins with 24 carrots.

Where did the Easter Bunny learn how to ski?

On the bunny hill.

How can you tell where the Easter Bunny has buried his treasure?

Eggs marks the spot!

Knock, knock.
Who's there?
Heidi.
Heidi who?

**Heidi the eggs all
around the yard!**

Why did the bunny go to the dance?

To do the bunny hop.

What is the end of Easter?

The letter "r."

What happens when you tickle an egg?

It cracks up.

What did the carrot say to the bunny rabbit?

Do you want to grab a bite?

Why shouldn't you ever eat an Easter egg who's a shoddy comedian?

All of their yolks are bad.

What day does an Easter egg hate the most?

Fry-day.

What do bunnies sing at birthday parties?

Hoppy birthday to you!

How does the Easter Bunny travel?

By Hare-Plane.

Why did the Easter Bunny not attend his family dinner?

He didn't want to go because he was having a bad hare day.

What does the Easter Rabbit get for making a basket?

Two points just like everybody else!

What kind of books do bunnies read?

Ones with hoppy endings!

**What do ducks
have for lunch?**

Soup and quackers.

What do you call the Easter Bunny when he has fleas?

Bugs Bunny.

**Why is a bunny
the luckiest animal
in the world?**

It has four rabbits' feet.

**How do you make
a bunny stew?**

**You keep him waiting
for three hours.**

What did the Easter Bunny say to the carrot who was moving away?

Been nice gnawing you.

How do you make Easter easier?

Replace the "*t.*" with an "*i*"!

What do you call a bunny Transformer?

Hop-timus Prime.

What do you call rabbits that live at the North Pole?

Cold.

Would February March?

No, but April May.

What do you get when you cross a bumblebee with the Easter Bunny?

A honey bunny.

What did the Easter Bunny say to his smart sister?

Stop being such an egghead!

What do you call a bunny with money?

A millionhare.

What kind of bean can't grow in a garden?

A jelly bean.

What activity do a lot of Easter eggs enjoy with their families?

They love singing kara-yolk-e.

What do you say to the Easter Bunny on his birthday?

Hoppy birthday!

What do Easter eggs drink in the morning?

Egg-spressos.

What sports team was the Easter egg on in school?

The runny team.

Why should you go to an Easter Bunny whenever you run into a problem?

They're all ears.

What's an Easter egg's favorite motivational phrase?

Stay on the sunny side up!

What would you call an Easter Bunny who's smiling all the time?

Hoppy.

Why does Peter Cottontail hop down the bunny trail?

Because he is too young to drive.

What did the Easter Bunny's mother say when she realized he was late for school?

You need to hop to it.

Why was the father Easter egg so strict?

He was hard boiled.

Where does the Easter Bunny get his eggs?

From an eggplant.

Why did the jelly bean go to school?

Because he really wanted to be a Smartie.

Why did the Easter Bunny throw the clock out the window?

He wanted to see time fly.

Why can't a rabbit's nose be twelve inches long?

Because then it would be a foot.

What proof is there that carrots are good for the eyes?

You don't see rabbits wearing eyeglasses.

What did the Easter Bunny say to his Easter egg helpers?

Let's hatch a plan to get things done!

Why do we paint Easter eggs?

Because it's easier than wallpapering them.

What kind of vegetable is angry?

A steamed carrot!

How many hairs in a rabbit's tail?

None, they're all on the outside.

What kind of bunny can't hop?

A chocolate one!

Which side of the Easter Bunny has the most fur?

The outside.

Who is the Easter Bunny's favorite movie actor?

Rabbit Downey, Jr.

Why did the bunnies go on strike?

They wanted a raise in celery!

What do you get when you cross a rabbit with an oyster?

The oyster bunny.

What do you call the Easter Bunny after a hard day's work?

Tired.

What did the bunny say when he only had thistles to eat?

Thistle have to do!

How do Easter chicks leave a building?

By the emergency egg-sit.

How is a rabbit like a cornstalk?

They both have big ears.

Which bunnies were famous bank robbers?

Bunny and Clyde!

Why does the Easter Bunny love Woodstock?

It's already tie-dyed.

What grows between your nose and chin?

Tulips.
(two lips)

What's invisible and smells like carrots?

Bunny farts.

**Where did the
Easter Bunny go
for a new tail?**

To a retail store.

What happened when 100 hares got loose on Main Street?

The police had to comb the area.

Where is the best place to learn about Easter eggs?

The hen-cyclopedia!

What's yellow, has long ears, and grows on trees?

The Easter Bun-ana.

What did the nice Easter egg always say before asking someone to move?

Egg-scuse me.

What was the Easter egg's reaction when he realized he had won the egg hunt?

He felt egg-static.

How did the Easter Bunny's family travel to meet him on Easter day?

They traveled via hare-plane.

Where did the smart Easter Bunny do his undergraduate degree in medicine?

He studied at Johns Hop-kins.

How does the Easter Bunny paint all the Easter eggs?

He hires Santa's elves during the offseason.

What do you call ten rabbits marching backward?

A receding hareline.

Waitress, what's this hare doing in my soup?

Looks like the backstroke.

How do you catch a unique bunny?

UNIQUE UP ON IT!

Why did the Easter Bunny have to fire the duck?

He kept quacking the eggs.

How can you make Easter preparations go faster?

Use the eggs-press lane.

What kind of jewelry is the best Easter gift?

A 14-carrot necklace.

Why did the baby chick cross the road?

To meet up with her Peeps.

What do you get when you pour hot water into a rabbit hole?

Hot cross bunnies.

How does an Easter Bunny keep his fur looking so good?

Hare spray.

What kind of rabbit tells jokes?

A funny bunny.

What did one Easter egg say to the other?

Heard any good yolks today?